Decorative
STENCILLING

Decorative
STENCILLING

KATRINA HALL
LAURENCE LLEWELYN-BOWEN

MEREHURST

For all our mothers, Stephanie, Patricia, Diana and Ellen

Published in 1994 by Merehurst Limited
Ferry House, 51–57 Lacy Road, Putney, London SW15 1PR
© Copyright 1994 Merehurst Limited

ISBN 1 85391 320 0

A catalogue record for this book is available from the British Library.

Edited by **Miren Lopategui**
Designed by **Lisa Tai**
Photography by **Jon Bouchier**

Typesetting by J&L Composition Ltd, Filey, North Yorkshire
Colour separation by Global Colour
Printed in Italy by Amilcarepizzi

Contents

Introduction

DESPITE CHANGING FASHIONS AND TECHNICAL improvements, stencilling – one of the most ancient design techniques – remains immensely popular with professional decorators and home improvers alike. In one form or another, it's still the technique most commonly used for producing patterns in quantity: the repeated application of pigment, paint or ink through a stiff board or template cut through with a design has created many of the world's most beautiful fabrics and wallpapers.

It's easy to understand why stencilling is so popular. Like most good ideas, it is simple – no specialist equipment or previous experience is necessary, and only one basic pattern is required.

There is also no end to its uses, whether for unifying the design scheme in an entire room, or adding that extra finishing touch to the most ordinary of objects in your home. You can use it on anything, ranging from the tiniest of boxes to a cushion, or lampshade – even a window.

The flexibility of stencilling can be seen by a quick glance at the history of interior decoration. Over 2,000 years ago, the ancient Egyptians were already using ordered, geometric stencils to create magnificent borders in their tombs and palaces. In the 10th century AD, the Chinese cut more intricate stencils to make dense, closely repeating patterns covering entire walls, while in 13th-century Europe, the jewel-like painted interiors of the Gothic cathedrals would have been impossible to achieve without the use of a stencil.

Although stencilling enjoyed a Victorian Gothic revival in England in the middle of the 19th century, it was in 18th-century America that it really became raised to an art form. Previously, stencilled finishes had been retouched to make them look more like freehand paintings, or polished up so that the final effect was closer to block-printed wallpaper. But the homesteaders of the 18th-century American colonies understood that the slightly patchy, often rough, finish left by the paint applied through the stencil had its own design possibilities.

The stencilled room

Despite being completely abreast of European fashions, the early Americans were a three-month voyage away from the furnishings, papers and fabrics of Paris and London. So, as with their furniture styles, they re-interpreted fashionable forms and executed them with local materials and craftsmen, or, in more far-flung communities, did it all themselves. This approach and style latterly became known as 'colonial', with regional variations such as 'French Colonial' around New Orleans; 'Neo Dutch' in New York; 'New England' and, of course, Shaker. However, since the Shakers – a strict, religious order – believed all forms of decoration to be frivolous, and therefore ultimately the work of Lucifer, any instances of Shaker stencils are devilishly rare.

THE PRESENT DAY

Between us we must have stencilled just about anything that can take a coat of paint, from light

fittings to chairbacks; restaurant walls to shop ceilings; glass doors to sea grass floors – and even, when required by theatrical productions – the odd naked body or two. In the commercial world, there's a strongly held belief that stencilling is a costly and difficult technique, which means that it's not often used in large commercial contracts. From experience we have found this to be completely untrue, and in fact will often deliberately choose stencilling over more generally favoured options such as wallpaper. We have always found that by cutting and designing our own stencils, we can exercise complete control over the pattern, colour and form of the decorations. When using wallpapers produced by another designer there is obviously always some element of fitting a scheme around their repeats and colours, which inevitably leads to unsuccessful compromises.

Used on a smaller scale, in the home, stencilling really comes into its own. Unlike many other decorative techniques, it is neither time-consuming nor complicated, and, provided your stencil paint is compatible with the surface you are stencilling (see page 34), you can start almost immediately. Working in the commercial world, deadlines are all-important, which means that schemes must be simple in order to be done quickly. We have, therefore, ensured that all the projects in this book meet the standards of economy, simplicity and durability to which we, as professionals, have to be committed.

From the course of our work and long experience, we can say there are several golden rules to adhere to. The first is, never skimp on the early

professional designers as too expensive – or difficult – and therefore unrealistic for your purposes. By sitting down and really analysing how the look has been achieved, you will quickly see – as we did – that even the most complicated interiors are based upon variations of quite basic combinations of pattern, form and colour.

The American settlers should be very much taken as a role model here. Like all of us, they must have looked at sumptuously illustrated pattern books (their equivalent of our glossy interiors magazines) and dreamt of how wonderful it would be to have rare and beautiful patterned silks, and velvety-soft flocked wallpapers in their homes. Cost and logistics made owning the originals impossible, so they learnt to achieve the same effects by cutting stencils from the fabulous patterns of the originals, and then letting their imaginations run riot. With just a little flair and some considered thinking, anyone can turn their own dream scheme into reality.

stages. Time spent in developing your stencil design, and analysing its shape, scale, and repeat (not to mention the colour scheme) will dramatically increase your chances of success.

You will soon find yourself creating stunning results with the minimum of effort, but even this tiny amount of effort will require enough commitment and seriousness to see the job through. So, if you're a first-time stenciller, start small and with a clear diary. Over-estimate the time it's going to take you to complete the project, and then prepare yourself to be pleasantly surprised when you finish ahead of schedule.

Finally, don't be too easily put off. Flicking through glossy interior design magazines, it's all too easy to dismiss the elegant effects employed by

Equipment and Materials

The wide range of stencilling equipment on the market will leave most would-be stencillers spoilt for choice. For those who prefer specialist stencilling kits and paints, these are also available. They can be a real confidence boost if you are a beginner, but more down-to-earth materials will achieve the same effects – and may well work out cheaper!

Equipment and materials

IF YOU ARE STENCILLING FOR THE FIRST TIME, you may well be tempted to go for commercially produced pre-cut stencils and specialist paints and crayons – or even some of the complete stencilling kits that are now available in many art or decorating shops. This has obvious advantages, but there can be a down side too. Ready-made kits may work out

There is a wide variety of commercially produced ready-made stencils on the market. Although handy for the beginner, they can work out expensive.

Oiled manila card, the traditional choice for stencilling.

expensive, and the constraints of using an inherited design can limit your creativity. And while it is true that there are many specialist paints around – even ones that are specially designed for stencilling on fabrics, tiles and china – they often involve complicated processes using stabilisers, fixers and the like. The other thing to remember with these products is that they are very brand-based. Often hijacked by the marketing departments the label can often end up more 'hard sell' than 'how-to'.

It's not necessary to buy these specialist products for successful stencilling – there can be no doubt that exactly the same effects can be easily achieved with more down-to-earth materials – but for many people who are starting out, specialist paints or crayons may understandably offer a confidence boost that overrides all other considerations. For those preferring the 'do-it-yourself' approach, the main equipment to buy is as follows:

STENCIL CARDS
These fall into several types:
Oiled manila card is the traditional choice for stencilling. It is available from most well-stocked art shops, though a quick ring around might be advisable in more far-flung areas to save a wasted journey. Manila card, while extremely tough and durable, is surprisingly easy to cut. (It also has a very particular heady smell that derives from the linseed oil used in its manufacture.) However, the sheets are often a little on the small side (somewhere between A3 and A2 – probably some long-forgotten Imperial standard) – which can be frustrating for large repeats, since joined pieces never have the same resilience as a whole sheet. Although manila card is not wildly expensive, it may be an idea to always try and place your stencil economically within the sheet, so that off-cuts can be used for other, smaller projects.

Acetate sheets have one major advantage over manila card. They are see-through, which makes it easy to see exactly what you are doing as you go along. This means that any dribbles or unfortunate smudges can be spotted as they occur, and dealt with before they have time to dry or harden. It's also useful when working on complicated repeating patterns or additional colours, since positioning the stencil in relation to the design can be done by eye. As a plastic, acetate is the most durable stencilling material available. Like manila card, it can be bought from art shops, but do be prepared to dig around since it's known under a variety of trade names and sold for a variety of uses. Any sensible art shop will, however, know exactly what you want if you take time to explain what you want it for. The toughness that makes acetate extremely attractive for a large stencilling project unfortunately means that it is not the most sympathetic material to cut. A sharp blade can follow even the most intricate of cuts successfully but acetate's smooth surface will make slipping blades an occupational hazard. The extra care needed in cutting should, however, be offset against the positive advantage of being able to cut your pattern straight from the design by placing the acetate directly over the original drawing and cutting line for line. Once cut, acetate is without doubt the best stencil for awkward corners as it can be bent easily while remaining stiff enough to leave even the finest of details intact.

Plan trace cannot be praised enough. As its name suggests, this is, effectively, tracing paper. It has all the best properties of both acetate and manila card, being easily cut, translucent and extremely durable. Added to this, it has the unique and extremely useful advantage of being suitable for use in a photocopier. This means that you can have your design copied directly on to the trace. During this process, the drawing can be blown up or reduced to fit a specific space or the image multiplied to make a repeating pattern. (If you can't track down a local photocopier you can cut your pattern line for line as with acetate.) Being thinner than manila or acetate, plan trace will give your finished design beautifully crisp, neat outlines. And, despite being so tough that it cannot be torn, it offers enough friction for a sharp blade to be easily controlled, thus minimizing the risk of inadvertent slipping. Inevitably for such a wonder product, plan trace is just a little bit more difficult to find and may cost slightly more than either manila card or acetate. Larger art shops should stock it and anyone listed under graphic suppliers in the telephone book will doubtless have some tucked away.

Above Cutting line for line is a major advantage of both acetate and plan trace.

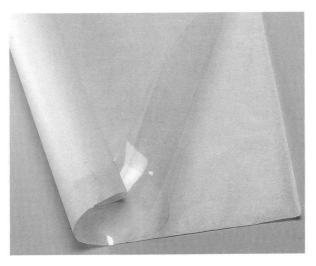

Far left Acetate is extremely tough and durable and is much valued for commercial stencilling projects.

Left Plan trace is the ideal medium for stencilling, combining the qualities of both manila and acetate.

CUTTING TOOLS

You will soon find that with the wrong equipment, cutting a stencil can be one of the most laborious, stressful and uncomfortable pursuits ever known. The only way to make the process easier is to use a sharp cutting tool. This means not only starting off with a sharp blade, but taking pains to change it regularly for a fresh one the minute cutting your stencil becomes heavy going. Beyond that, the choice of blade holder is a matter of personal comfort. Obviously, large craft knives such as **Stanley knives** with their thick blades, while ideal for consistent straight cuts, are not suited to intricate patterns. Of the multitude of other craft knives available, the best are usually those which can be comfortably held like a pen. The top end of the market has to be the round shafted knives that take scalpel blades. These are comfortable to use and are perfect for cutting tight corners and sharp details. The next step down would be the flat-handled craft knives with retractable, disposable blades. They can, however, be as unwieldy as a Stanley knife with the added disadvantage of small blades that break easily under sideways pressure. It is at the lower end of the market that you will find the most flexible cutting tool.

Scalpel Once you have conquered your initial shock at wielding such a frighteningly surgical implement, scalpels have a long, graceful blade that is a joy to steer. They come in a range of handle shapes and sizes – most art shops will now have a display of blades and handles. Hooked, crooked, or parrot-beaked blades are not appropriate for cutting stencils. Opt instead for the medium to fine equilateral triangle-shaped blades. Consult the sales assistant before committing yourself, however, since various blades are designed to fit specific handles and no amount of adhesive tape will make a large blade firm on a small handle.

Scissors There are some patterns, such as simple star shapes or large flowing designs, where sharp pointed scissors can be used successfully. The shock given to the stencil when puncturing the card can, however, make permanent creases that will make using the stencil difficult. Scissors are nothing like as easy to control as a knife and mask much of the line you wish to follow as you use them.

Pinking shears can be used to create a decorative saw-tooth edge. They are really only at their best, however, when used for long straight runs. The relative smallness of the zig-zag edge can look just plain messy when seen from a distance but for smaller objects seen at close range, they can offer some interesting stencilled effects.

PAINTS

Having already covered commercially produced paints specifically formulated for stencilling, an investigation into less costly and more widely available alternatives should be considered.

Emulsion Ordinary household emulsion has much to recommend it in that it's easy to get hold of and offers an almost infinite choice of colours. Emulsion is a latex-based water-soluble paint and

Of the wide variety of craft knives available, scalpels are the best suited for stencilling projects.

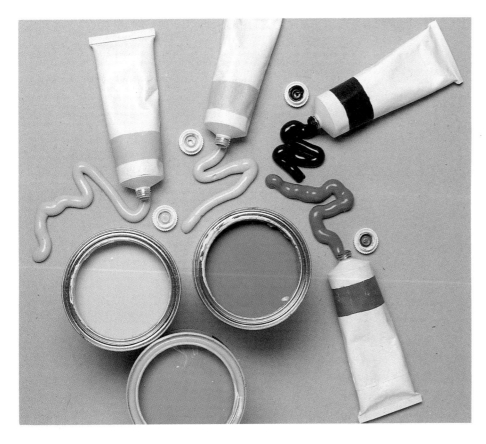

Left Household emulsion paint is available in two finishes: vinyl silk, with a slight sheen, and vinyl matt.

Below Stencilling a design in vinyl silk on to a matt base of the same colour.

Stencilling projects can be undertaken with household paint or artist's paint colours, as shown here.

as such is easy to handle and not difficult to remove from brushes provided they are rinsed immediately after use. It offers two finishes: matt and vinyl silk. The former gives a surface similar to old-fashioned distemper without the unstable powdery chalkiness; the latter leaves a similar effect to traditional oil paints with their discreet sheen. Many companies produce emulsion in very small tins (250ml) as colour testers, which are usually an ideal size for most stencilling projects.

Stencilling with emulsion, whether vinyl silk or matt, can be a little tricky to begin with. Launching straight into a tin will doubtless mean you end up forcing too much paint through the stencil leaving a smudged and messy pattern not readily recognizable even to its own designer. The simple solution is to call into play the paint reservoir (see page 19). Given this means of regulating the paint flow, many interesting effects can be achieved by off-

setting vinyl silk and matt emulsions. Stencilling a design in a slightly darker shade of vinyl silk on to a matt base of the same colour can give you effects similar to rich damasks or brocades. Alternatively, by isolating and stencilling one element in vinyl silk, you can lend an exciting feeling of movement to the overall design as the light is reflected by the paint's slight sheen.

Artist's Acrylic Paints From experience, acrylic is the most flexible and manageable option. All art shops now stock acrylic paints since they have to a large extent overtaken the former popularity of oil paints amongst amateur artists. When standing in your local art shop confronted by a variety of paint displays you will normally find four types of paint on sale: oil, acrylic, alkyd and gouache. Sometimes alkyd, acrylic and gouache get jumbled up, in which case make sure you don't leave the shop with a tube or pot of gouache or any other

Artist's acrylic paints come in a wide variety of stunning colours.

paint referred to as watercolour or poster paint. Not only are these paints water-soluble, they will remain so after you have finished the project.

Following years of research, acrylic paints are now manufactured to be immensely hard-wearing and fade-resistant, and come in a staggering range of colours, including fluorescent, pearlescent and metallic finishes. The main advantage of using acrylics for stencilling is that you can control the paint's consistency and texture straight from the tube. Undilute, acrylic paint is much 'harder' and 'drier' than emulsion, which will create interesting textured finishes with a brush or sponge. Used neat, you will find that it dries almost instantly on the wall. This has the advantage of minimizing the risk of damaging your design when moving your stencil, but inevitably means that smudges and other mistakes are impossible to remove. For more subtle, slightly transparent effects, a little water in the mixture will soften the finish. Be warned that acrylic's fast-drying properties can have disastrous and irreparable effects on brushes and sponges left out of water.

Acrylic paints are not generally produced in the subtle shades most of us like to use in home decoration. You will therefore have to be prepared to mix colours to achieve the right hue (see pp. 32–3). Frustratingly, the cost of using acrylics can mount up as you may have to buy several tubes of paint to achieve the right shade.

Alkyd paints are a comparatively recent range that have been formulated to provide many of the qualities of oil paints with as rapid a drying time as acrylic. Alkyd colours are thinned with white spirit or turps which is necessary to make their 'buttery' texture suitable for stencilling.

Oil Paints For the purist or revivalist there can be no choice other than oil paints. They are, however, the trickiest paint to use for stencilling and dry extremely slowly. For those who have mastered how to apply them and have a good idea of the ideal paint consistency for stencilling, oil paint mixed with a little varnish or oil painting medium can be used to create beautiful transparent effects. Extreme care must be taken in removing the stencil after applying paint, however, since oil pigments remain unstable for a minimum of four hours, which could lead to smudges if you are clumsy. (Any such horrors can be easily 'erased' with a clean rag or cotton bud, however, as long as the mistake is small and close to an element of the design with which you are happy.) Unlike other paints, oils can be used on nearly every surface except the obvious paint repellors such as laminates, glass, ceramics and unprimed metals. You won't find

Artist's oil paints are ideal for subtle or earthy tones.

Far left *As yet, the choice of colours available in spray paints is quite limited. Mixing colours can only be achieved with successive sprays.*

Left *Masking the area around the stencil is essential to prevent overspray from the paint jet.*

many of the bright colours offered by acrylics but, for mellow earth tones or smoky shades, they are difficult to beat. Like acrylic, building up a palette of colours with them can be costly.

Spray Paints A comparatively recent addition to the stenciller's armoury, spray paints are ideal for those who find hand-applied methods difficult to master. So-called craft sprays are available from art, craft and model shops in an increasing but still limited colour range. While these are appropriate for most surfaces, you would need to call upon the impregnable finish offered by car sprays if you want to stencil on surfaces such as glass, ceramics or metals. Even then, car sprays are not recommended for use on objects which are cleaned regularly or that suffer boisterous, heavy wear. Of all the paints discussed, car sprays have the most limited colour range which can lead to rather frantic colour schemes based around Cortina Red with highlights of Escort Blue. They are also highly toxic and must only be used in well ventilated conditions with a face mask. Inhaling deeply in a closed room where car spray has just been used will give your lungs a very good idea of how the ozone layer feels.

Whether using a car spray or craft spray, you must be careful to spray a very fine layer – almost a dusting – through the stencil. Applying too much

paint will lead to immediate runs and dribbles – a particular hazard with car spray, which has a long hardening or drying time. The only way of achieving a light paint layer is to hold the can as far from the stencil as possible. This, of course, means that you run the risk of spraying not only through the stencil but around the stencil as well. It's a good idea in such cases to make a scrap paper mask. This is not difficult and will prove invaluable in protecting adjacent finishes.

The only way to mix spray colours is to use successive, very lightly sprayed coats. Since the paint hits the wall in minute pin prick spots, it is by offsetting one colour spot against another that different hues are achieved, just like a television screen where all the colours are only arrived at by differing densities of tiny red, green and blue dots.

Finally, for those whose commitment to the environment forbids the propulsion of paint courtesy of CFCs there are do-it-yourself spray alternatives. Large, cumbersome and noisy air compressors can be leased from most hire shops. But, while great fun for painting an entire room all one colour in 60 seconds flat, they are too meaty a machine for most stencilling projects. Smaller air guns like those used by artists commissioned to produce record sleeves for heavy rock groups may be ideal for stencilling, but they are an expensive commit-

Colour mixing with spray paint, when looked at close up, closely resembles the spots of colour on a TV screen.

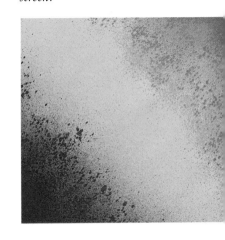

ment. More basic models will be cheaper. Powered by as much air as you can pump with the rubber bladder, they create a gentle focused spray that is excellent for intricate or delicate stencils or for subtle graduations of colour. They fit most felt-tip pens, but should obviously not be used with art pens that are water-soluble, otherwise your work will not prove very permanent.

PAINT APPLICATORS

Applying any paint through a stencil with a small man-made sponge applicator (see page 19) has many advantages. It is quick, cheap and disposable. However, it will not give you the same control or offer such a wide variety of effects as a brush.

Brushes specifically designed for stencilling have short, stiff hairs. Available from art and craft shops, they can sometimes be found in traditional hardware stores or paint merchants. As befits such a specialist tool, stencil brushes constitute one of the biggest financial commitments to the would-be stenciller. It is possible, however, to use ordinary decorator's paint brushes: 2.5cm (1in), 5cm (2in),

7.5cm (3in) brushes are best. Man-made bristles are less flexible than exotic, luxuriously soft badger hair and work better.

Nothing beats a proper stencil brush, but you can adapt an ordinary brush to make it more efficient, by binding the brush or cutting it down (see below).

As a finishing touch a rag or sponge dipped in drying paint will give a direct imprint that can be used as an interesting random effect over a more opaque application of colour.

RUBBER GLOVES

Whatever your chosen technique, stencilling has the unfortunate side-effect of leaving as much pigment on your hands as on the wall. So, unless you're prepared to spend the next week with permanently painted fingers, you would be best advised to wear rubber gloves when applying the paint. Standard household rubber gloves can be very cumbersome. The best alternative is surgical gloves which can be bought from larger chemist's or medical suppliers.

Stencilling brushes have characteristically short stubby hairs. Though not ideal, ordinary household brushes can be adapted to meet these needs.

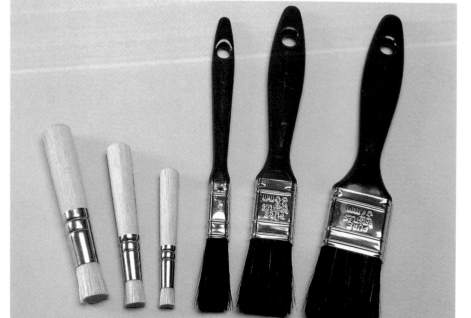

Tightly bind a strip of masking tape about a third of the way down the bristles to make them stiff.

Alternatively, bind the bristles as above, then cut the bristles by cutting through the tape.

Making your own stencil and paint applicator

If you would like to ease yourself into stencilling gently, without buying more specialized equipment, you can make your own stencil using an empty cereal packet and ordinary household emulsion paint. This is also ideal for trying out a complicated pattern in rough.

Using wet paint on ordinary uncoated card will eventually leave you with a soggy mess, which is why the waxed card of the cereal packet is ideal. You will, however, need to waterproof the inner,

Cut out a simple outline from the cereal packet using a pair of embroidery scissors or an extremely sharp craft knife.

Pour emulsion paint into a saucer covering it by about one third. Add a dribble of water and gently mix together, then squeeze the reservoir sponge firmly into the paint until it has taken up most of the mixture. Dab the smaller applicator sponge on to the reservoir until this too has taken up the paint. Then use the applicator to paint the stencil.

non-waxed side with a quick coat of any household varnish to protect it from the paint. The pulp used to make most packages and boxes these days is never of a high quality due mainly to the large proportions of recycled material companies now (most admirably) use. This means that highly complicated or detailed designs are virtually impossible, and even the simplest shapes must be cut with an extremely sharp craft knife or a pair of embroidery scissors.

Your own paint applicator can be made from a small square pad cut from an ordinary man-made kitchen sponge – the large, Swiss cheese-like holes of bath sponges will cause a disastrous build-up of paint. Simply cut off about a third of the sponge, depending on your design, and keep the rest to use as a paint reservoir. Paint reservoirs act rather like ink pads to help solve a major problem when stencilling: irregular flow of paint through the stencil. It's important to get this right. Too much paint and the design will smudge; too little and you will have only the most ghostly of patterns.

To prepare the paint, mix a tiny amount of water with some emulsion paint in an old saucer (you can easily soak the paint off later with detergent and hot water), then squeeze the reservoir sponge firmly into the paint until it has taken up most of the mixture. Gently dab with a small pad cut from the remaining sponge on to the reservoir until this too has taken up the paint, then dab it again on a clean sheet of newspaper or an uncut part of the stencil, to check that the paint isn't oozing or dribbling. A clean crisp imprint of the sponge means that you are ready to start stencilling. You can then continue to use your applicator to paint your stencil, building up the density of paint as you go along, and following the techniques described on page 34. This is stencilling at its easiest and most basic – perfect for a quick try-out.

Techniques

Decorative stencilling techniques are easy to master and, once learnt, will act as a springboard to help you create your own patterns and motifs. There may be a great deal of planning and preparation in the initial stages, but the net result – a unique and individually conceived design – will be infinitely more rewarding than anything you can ever buy in a shop!

Designing your stencil

IT'S NOW TIME TO START MAKING SOME BIG decisions. At this stage, you will probably have an exact image of the finished project at the back of your mind. But, inevitably, it's making this abstract germ of an idea into reality that, for many beginners and professionals alike, is one of the most daunting parts of the whole stencilling process.

First, think of the specific job your stencil design is aiming to do. One of the most effective uses of stencilling is to provide 'accents' of pattern or colour that can bridge a gap between, say, your curtain furnishing fabric or upholstery. You can do this by repeating an existing pattern on objects such as lampshades or mirror frames, or with repeated details running around the perimeter of a room, as in a frieze or dado.

If you are a beginner the simplest and most direct starting point may be to literally 'lift' a design element that is already in your room – say, the curtains, or a cushion, or seat cover – by tracing it. When dealing with a large free form repeat with a variety of contrasting elements, this can seem daunting. So begin by flattening the design – draw the curtains, squeeze all the air from the cushion, or remove the cotton pads from the seat covers where the pattern is.

Having done this, stand back as far away from the pattern as space will allow and screw up your eyes until the overall design becomes a blur. You will soon notice some elements in the design are stronger and more dominant than others – perhaps because of the way they are drawn, the strength or

For most people, the first step to evolving their own stencil is to carefully trace the pattern of a fabric or wallpaper they already have in their home.

After tracing the design, the next step is to take out any small, fiddly or complicated shapes that might prove impossible to reproduce. Your aim should be to create a design that, while obviously derived from the original, uses only the most important shape.

depth of the colour used, or the darkness, or 'tonal value' of the motif. It is these dominant elements that will provide the framework to your pattern.

Once you have done this, you will then need to do some further editing, depending on the stencilling projects you have planned. A single pattern, such as an isolated motif on, say, a chair seat or tray, is simple to start with, since, as long as the scale is right, the motif won't need much reworking. If, on the other hand, you want to tackle a repeating stencil to border your room or a lampshade, it's best to focus on an element that spreads to either side of the design. Leaves or scrolls that stick out from a more densely patterned centre will give you more scope to link the space between each repeat. A nicely enclosed posy or symmetric element that leans heavily to one side, on the other hand, will be very difficult to repeat without adding other linking elements taken either from the allover pattern, or your own imagination.

TRACING THE DESIGN

Having chosen the starting point of your design, flatten out the pattern and trace it out accurately line for line. Bear in mind that a soft fibre tip felt pen or a very soft pencil are easier to manoeuvre on fabric than the spear-like points of biros or hard pencils. Spirit, magic or permanent markers may bleed through tracing paper so use them carefully. At this early stage, where you may find yourself with high levels of wastage, greaseproof paper or baking paper can be used as a more easily obtained and cheaper alternative to tracing paper or plan trace. Don't worry if you have to resort to this. Even professionals will try tracing a pattern several times to get the best outline, since it's inevitable that the tracing paper and traced pattern move as you draw, causing distortions in the design. You may find it helpful to include surrounding elements in your trace, even though at first glance they don't seem appropriate for inclusion. They may well prove useful as the design evolves.

Taking your carefully copied trace, sit down and think hard as to how it can be simplified. Analyse its overall shape and its most dominant elements. Then take another sheet of tracing paper and make a new copy, leaving out any smaller fiddly elements that might be impossible to reproduce. Your goal should be to create a design that, while obviously derived from the original, uses only the broader, flatter and more important shapes. For instance, a curving tendril of ivy complete with stalk and runners in the original can be effectively mirrored by simply concentrating on the broad pointed shapes of the leaves while completely ignoring the fiddly and fine line shapes that have been used to define the stalk. As long as the positioning of the leaves has been kept accurate, the gentle curve of the motif will still be maintained even without the extra detail.

NEGATIVE AND POSITIVE SPACE

You will now need to look at your traced design with a critical eye as to its practicality as a stencil. Most stencils use 'negative space' – i.e., it's the bit you cut out that creates the pattern. Obviously, that negative space must be completely surrounded by positive space – the uncut remainder of the stencil – so, focusing on each element, check that your design is surrounded by a constant border

Using a medium to thick marker, draw around the design to outline the areas that you will be cutting.

that will not be cut or broken by the intrusion of another shape. This is where you will have to start creating your own borders of 'filaments' to define a pattern. On a luscious bunch of grapes that in the original was given shape and form by different colours, you will have to rely on creating a filament that defines the shape of each grape. For something this detailed, think again on its suitability for your project. You may find that the same effect can be achieved by outlining the entire bunch and then defining the space between just a few of the grapes. The same applies to more complicated flower or leaf shapes. For your stencil to work properly, you will need a space of around 5mm (¼in) between each cut. Smaller filaments will not only break easily but can also allow paint to seep behind the stencil. Always try not to leave yourself with too many floating filaments. Just being joined at one end can make the filament liable to be wobbly enough to move as you apply the paint, or to become creased as you remove the stencil.

Having made sure that each negative space is constantly bordered by the positive, start mapping out where you want your filaments. By far the easiest way of drawing up the next stage is to follow the design line for line with an extremely thick marker pen. A wide nib will give you the thickness of each filament in one line, but make a mental note that when it comes to cutting, you must cut either side of the line rather than down the middle.

SCALING UP AND DOWN

It's now time to offer up the design so far and see how it looks in its final resting place. It may well be that it is too small or too big. This is very easy to solve with a quick trip to the nearest photocopier. Just take a ruler and measure the correct size you want your motif to be enlarged or reduced to. Photocopiers work on a rather complicated system of preset percentages, and you may find that you have to accept a copy that is not the exact measurement you wanted. Don't worry about this.

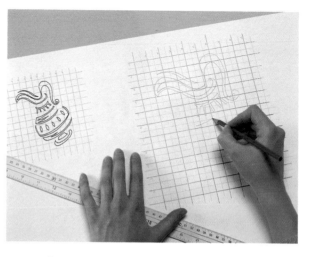

To double the size of any motif, draw a grid over the original. Then, by drawing another grid exactly double the first, you can transfer the design line for line using the squares as a point of reference.

It's very rare that a slightly undersized or oversized stencil doesn't work as well as one of the exact and correct dimensions. Always have one or two copies made either side of the correct size and keep any intermediate sized copies as you may well find them useful later. Also have a fistful of copies made of the right size so that you can play around with them when you get home, refining some shapes, losing others and trying out different colour combinations.

If photocopiers frighten the life out of you, there's another technique you can use for scaling up or down. This will involve a grid. Say, for example, your original is 20cm (8in) high and your finished stencil needs to be 40cm (16in) to fit comfortably on the surface you have prepared, the grid you draw over the original should have squares each measuring 1 × 1cm. On a separate sheet of paper draw another grid, each of whose squares is exactly double, that is 2 × 2cm. It will help if you draw the grid in ink, as you'll have to transfer the design free-hand from grid to grid, rubbing out mistakes. Then, by eye or with a ruler, assess the position of each line within the square. A line that cuts a square diagonally from corner to corner in the original can then be easily reproduced on the larger grid. Always start off by sketching in the overall shape of the pattern leaving any details until later. Go for simplified, perhaps even squared off, lines at first. You can always give them a more accurate shape later.

You are now left with the bare bones of your stencil. It's always a good idea to give yourself some time at this stage. Stick the stencil design in its intended position and use a critical eye to see how well it's going to work. During the early stages of simplification your design may have been left looking a little sparse. Alternatively, it may not have the right shape or outline for the intended effect. If your stencil is to repeat, now is the time to place two or three copies close together to see how the overall design will work. Tightening up your design now will require a little creativity and you may have to resort to basic collage skills learnt at primary school. If you find you have a particularly unsuccessful blank space, rummage back through the earlier stages of your design, paying particular attention to the photocopies you made that were under- or over-sized. The first stage trace should also be thoroughly raided, with particular thought given to the elements bordering the design in the original pattern. Cut out anything you feel may be useful and set to work playing around with your new-found palette of pattern elements. You'll be surprised at the results. What may have been an oversized vine leaf when you started out could now, through the expediencies of scale, fit exactly in an unsightly blank space. If you come across an element that's both the right size and the right shape, but pointing in the wrong direction, don't forget that tracing it and reversing the paper will give you an exact mirror image. You might even find yourself returning to the original at this stage to find additional elements to pep up the design. When you have the effect you want, reach out for the glue, and stick your design down on to paper.

It is now time to make the final copy. You could always photocopy the paste-up and leave it at that, but a fresh trace is invariably a good idea to keep the lines nice and clean and to help you refine the design further.

To polish up any design, re-assembling offcuts or unwanted preliminary drawings will help in filling blank spaces or balancing the look of the motif.

Practised stencillers know the value of a clean-lined final design to follow when cutting the stencil. This is best achieved by making a final trace of the design.

Clean, flowing lines are normally a sign of confidence; an insecure draughtsman will tend to draw lines in small broken strokes, particularly if using a hardish pencil or biro. If you feel apprehensive, it may help to make a tracing of your design with a very soft pencil, felt tip pen or small watercolour brush dipped in ink. By using tracing paper you won't be marking or damaging the original and can therefore allow yourself to loosen up. If you make a mess, all you need do is start again on new trace. As you build up speed and confidence, you will find that not only will the lines become more constant, but the design will start to achieve a flowing elegance that did not come across with your original disjointed pencil marks. For smaller, more intricate or detailed parts of the design, you will obviously need a sharper line. Even here, however, try, if possible, to use one line per element.

You now have your final design or, as it was known in the Renaissance, cartoon. One of the advantages of tracing paper is that you can now look at its mirror image by turning the paper over – an old trick much used by the Italian painters. By doing this, anything that doesn't quite come off will be much more apparent.

TRANSFERRING THE DESIGN

The final cartoon is now ready for another trip to the photocopier. This is not essential, but can offer valuable insurance if the worst should come to the worst during the cutting process. If plan trace is to be your chosen stencil medium, you can transfer the design straight on to a sheet at this stage via the photocopier. For those using acetate or plan trace, the original should now be fixed under the stencil and cutting commenced line for line. If transferring your design on to manila card, there are four methods you can use. The first is to draw up a size-for-size grid similar to that described earlier for rescaling the design. This means redrawing the design more or less free-hand but with a

grid to give you the essential points of reference. This inevitably leads to fuzzy lines which you will curse when it comes to cutting, but going over the first pencil lines with a heavy felt tip will help.

The second method, though labour-intensive, is great fun and interesting, in that it was the favoured method in the Italian Renaissance. To follow in Leonardo da Vinci's footsteps you will need to follow each line of your design with a series of pin pricks, pushing holes through the cartoon on to a separate piece of paper. You will need to judge the distance between the holes carefully. Too far apart and they will only leave the barest of impressions. Too close and you will end up perforating the

By following the lines of a design with a map pin, and pricking through on to the stencil card, you will be able to subsequently cut the lines with a knife.

design like a book of stamps. Needles and pins tend to be too fine for this exercise; mapping pins, with their stout heads and long sharp points, make the best, neatly rounded holes. Provided both design and card are well anchored together, you can then prick your design straight through on to the manila. A more faithful transfer can be achieved by rubbing charcoal through the pin pricks on to the card below – use a piece of cotton wool to really force the powdery charcoal through. This method is ideal if you want to repeat the design in series, because the time taken in pricking through is a one-off and any number of transfers can be made with the small amount of effort required to apply the charcoal.

For most people, the simplest technique is to liberally shade the back of the design with a very soft pencil and trace the design with a harder pencil or biro. On darker manila cards this kind of pencil transfer can be a little difficult to see, and you may have to resort to good old-fashioned carbon paper which will give you a nice crisp and easy-to-see line.

With all these methods, and indeed the earlier tracing stages, always make sure that neither the design nor the trace nor the card can move and distort the image. Also, make sure the tape, glue or pins you are using to keep the two elements together are easy to remove and will not mark, tear or damage the surface.

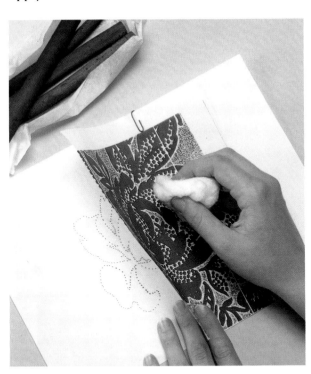

Charcoal rubbed through the holes pricked on the design will create an exact trace of the original.

Carbon paper gives the most direct impression of the original design. Typewriter carbon as opposed to plain carbon is paradoxically more sensitive and therefore more suitable for this use.

Cutting the stencil

WHEN YOU HAVE TRANSFERRED THE DESIGN ON to your chosen medium, you are ready to cut. The ideal surface for cutting a stencil is a self-healing rubber cutting mat – obviously, since cutting through paper and card you are more than likely to cut the surface underneath. Cutting mats are expensive, however, and adequate stand-ins can be found in unwanted vinyl floor tiles, the underside of rubber-backed carpet tiles, several sheets of heavy weight card or the covers of unwanted hard-backed books or glossy magazines. Start with intricate or fiddly shapes, since cutting these tends to pull at the card. If you start with long or flat areas, you may find that long filaments will distort or even tear as you cut adjacent small sections. A helpful tip is to stick the card to the cutting surface with spray adhesive before starting. It's generally a lot easier to cut towards yourself and, provided that you keep your knife as close to upright as possible, you are unlikely to slip and inadvertently commit hara-kiri. Always keep your free hand behind the cutting blade if you want to steady the stencil. Some longer lines are best cut if the knife is kept in a constant position and the stencil is moved. You will find this makes the process much less tiring and increases the flow of curved lines. Don't feel that each shape needs to be cut exactly as drawn – short cuts within the shape minimize effort. With a sharp blade you should need to exert the bare minimum of pressure. If you find yourself having to attack the stencil with psycho-like force, it probably means your blade has become blunt and will need to be changed.

Smaller, thinner blade handles such as scalpels will inevitably become uncomfortable after a while. A good tip is to increase the size of the handle

For curved or flowing shapes, keeping the blade steady while moving the card will give a more consistent cut.

Scalpel handles can become uncomfortable. In such cases, adding adhesive tape will increase the size of the shaft, making it easier to hold.

Mend broken filaments with a piece of masking tape cut to fit the damaged area.

with a liberal wrapping of adhesive tape. Not only will this make the knife easier to hold, it will also give you a more accommodatingly soft handle. Take care not to bind the blade to the handle since you will have to be able to change your blade when necessary.

Having cut the design into the stencil, cut the stencil itself down to a more usable size. If the design is to fit a specific area, it's a good idea to cut the stencil to fit exactly. For a repeating border underneath a picture rail or cornice, the top edge of the stencil must be exactly square to stop the design wobbling or running out as you follow the bottom edge of the moulding. Marking the middle line of the stencil will make it much easier to position. Regardless of the shape of the design,

draw a square with a ruler around the motif. By joining each corner diagonally, you will find the exact centre of the design where the lines meet. Using a set square or anything you know to be a true right angle, you can then mark off the vertical mid-line and horizontal mid-line.

If the design is for a repeating border, tracing one half of each of the neighbouring motifs either side of the stencil will help in lining up the stencil as you apply the paint. Broken or damaged filaments, or filaments accidentally sliced through as you cut can be mended with masking tape. Making a rough or oversized splint with the tape and then cutting the masking tape down to fit will ensure that you don't break the outlines around the damaged design.

Using colour

WITHOUT WISHING TO FRIGHTEN, UPSET OR PUT you had work could now be as nothing if the colour is not right. It's important to remember that stencilling as a decorative technique is a fundamentally flat finish. Simple, often harsh outlines can become simpler and most definitely harsher if the stencil and ground colours offer too strong a contrast. The most successful stencils are without doubt the subtler ones where the design is applied in a colour closely related to surrounding paint finishes. There can be no doubt that stencilling looks at its best over a mellowed paint finish. This will immediately remove any anticipated problems of hardness and make sure your stencil doesn't end up looking as unsightly as a tattoo.

In an existing room scheme you will have a good idea of a colour you wish to either match or complement. Whatever your chosen stencil paint, it's always advisable to isolate the chosen colour on a paint manufacturer's chart or card. Even when

The texture of objects can drastically affect the way a colour looks.

mixing your own colours, you will still find this point of reference extremely useful.

TAKING A COLOUR DIRECTLY FROM AN EXISTING PATTERN

Above all, remember that a colour in, say, a fabric or carpet has infinite variations as the light and shade hit each thread. What may appear a beautiful subtle faded old rose on a curtain can often turn out to be shocking flamingo as a painted finish. This is because the flat surface of the paint will reflect light uniformly, whereas the comparatively rough surface of fabric or even wallpaper disrupts reflection, thereby mellowing the colour. It is therefore an extremely good idea, having matched the exact pink from your curtains, to in fact use a shade that is several degrees lighter. This is very easy to do from a paint chart or colour card where different strengths of the same colour are given.

Having said a 'lighter colour', it is, in fact, far more complicated than that, as your chosen lighter pink will not be the same pink as the curtains but will have added white. The subtle shades used in

The three 'primary colours' – red, yellow and blue – can be arranged in a wheel. The area between each primary then provides 'secondary colours'; for example, yellow mixed with blue creates green, etc.

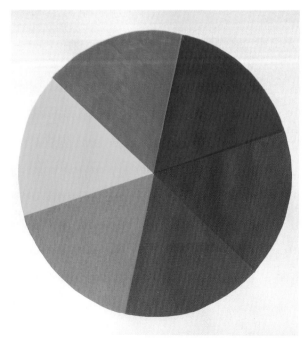

interior decoration achieve their subtlety from a surprising formulation of colours. So, the nicest pinks are rarely just red and white but can verge from blue to orange.

COMPLEMENTARY COLOURS

Over the last thousand years, artists have striven ceaselessly to produce naturalistic representations of colours in painting. But what appears to be a green leaf will in fact be made up of a variety of other hues from the yellows to blues and reds. By analysing the colours of natural objects and the way they appear to change in different lights, the theory of 'complementary colours' was evolved. This basically means that every single colour has an exact opposite.

There are three key or primary colours from which every colour can be mixed: red, yellow and blue. Different degrees of each colour produce a multiplicity of shades, starting with the secondary colours, such as green and purple. These colours are achieved as each primary colour overlaps the other. So, thinking in terms of a rainbow, the area where red overlaps yellow becomes orange; yellow overlaps blue and becomes green, and blue overlaps red and becomes purple. As can be seen the relationships are circular, starting at red and finishing at red, leaving what is known as the 'colour wheel' (see illustration). Seeing colours as a wheel, colour theorists then noticed that each colour had an opposite. Thus red's opposite is green, blue's opposite is yellow and so on. Armed with this knowledge, understanding the intensity of colours becomes much easier. Some paint manufacturers will actually detail these relationships on their colour cards showing you, through an arrangement of letters and numbers for each paint's serial number, how much blue is in a green or how much yellow is in an orange. What becomes surprising is how much of a colour's opposite or complementary hue has been used to achieve the desired shade.

Back to the pink. The real subtlety of our shade is due to the addition of red's complementary colour, green. Not only does this darken the colour but it removes any harshness from the red. Theoretically, in perfectly balanced proportions, all complementary colours when mixed will achieve a uniform brown grey. But, used sparingly, they're the best way of controlling the original colour.

When talking about colour, the terms 'hue' and 'tone' should be defined. Colour refers literally to the colour as in its primary or secondary name, i.e. red. 'Hue' defines its balance, in terms of which other colour predominates, thus, a red with an orange hue would be a salmon pink. 'Tone' refers to how dark it is. Assessing the hue and tone of a colour can be difficult with all the distractions of a busy and highly coloured pattern. You can make a good start by isolating the colour to be matched with a frame of white paper. From this you will be able to see that your pink does indeed have not only a dash of orange but also the faintest suggestion of green.

When matching or evaluating a colour from an existing pattern, it's often a good idea to isolate the area with a white frame to block out adjacent motifs.

MIXING COLOURS

One of the biggest misconceptions is that neither black nor white are colours. True, used straight from the tin, they come across as a pure or dead flat finish. But when mixed in with other colours they will give a particular hue to the final mix that is derived from their original colour balance. Blacks can, for example, vary from brown to blue to green, whites from yellow to blue. This may all sound like nit-picking but, when you're trying to mix a particular colour – say, our pink – adding some blue-black to darken it may completely destroy the subtle balance of orange, red and yellow. By the same token, lightening a colour with pure blue white can overturn the established relationships and make the colour unsuccessfully chalky or even dingy. Some guidance is given on paint tubes in that whites known as 'Flake White' have a pinkish hue, Chinese White errs towards yellow, whereas Titanium White is quite blue. Lamp Black can be rather blue green and Ivory Black is very brown. Therefore Flake White would be ideal for lightening our pink, which is very warm, and Ivory Black perfect to make it darker. But don't launch straight in.

Mixing colours, like making the best pastry or the most successful mayonnaise, should be done slowly, and all the ingredients added gradually and mixed thoroughly before more is put in. A little water in acrylics and a little turps in oil will keep the paint pliable and easy to mix. A stiff brush is best as it will allow you to thoroughly squash the paint around. Always mix more than you need as remixing is incredibly difficult and, provided that the mixed paint is sealed with cling film you will find it will last for as long as you need it. No matter how small the job, paint kettles make ideal containers. Because they are wider than they are deep, they minimize shadow, allowing you to see more of your mixture in direct light.

When you feel good about the 'colour' and relatively happy about the 'hue' – perhaps having added a dash of the colour's complement to keep the whole thing subtle – you must assess the 'tone'. If your pink is now too dark for the effect you require, squeeze out some Flake White on a separate saucer or dish and to this add a little red. This will leave you with a mixture that is unlikely to upset the careful balance. Keep the new pigment quite wet and apply a dribble at a time. The same principle is applied to making the colour darker with black. Whatever your chosen technique, now is the time to step back, since all paints change colour from wet to dry, so, before committing yourself to your mixture, allow a small sample patch to dry fully. A small blob next to the desired colour on your paint chart is ideal.

Whites and blacks always have a strong colour bias which can affect the final hue when mixing colours from scratch.

Colours should always be mixed in wide bowls with low sides that will not cast shadows on to the mixture.

Whether mixing from scratch or tinting commercial paints, colour should be added slowly and mixed vigorously as you go along.

Even paints straight from the tin may not be as exciting in reality as they appeared on the chart. A couple of brush strokes on a piece of paper stuck to the stencil's final destination will give you a useful opportunity to make sure it is right. Tinting paints in the tin is not difficult and should be tackled using the same principles as mixing from scratch. Mix a really quite runny version of your tint and gradually add this to the paint mixing slowly as you go. You may find that trickling the tint down the inside of the tin will give you more flexibility and is easier to mix in than a huge blob right in the middle. It also means that you'll be left with a reservoir from which you can take small quantities. There is always a tremendous temptation to add the paint too quickly, since it's often only after subsequent mixings that the colour takes. Patience is most decidedly a virtue in this instance. As insurance, it is always a good idea to empty an approximate third from the tin just in case your mixing is heavy-handed to start with. By feeding in some of the original colour you have saved gradually, most mistakes can be rectified. When in your local paint merchants, resist the temptation to walk out with ready-mixed tints. They are extremely strong and have ruined more tins of paint in the hands of the impatient than can be imagined.

Most paints, whether oil, acrylic or emulsion, can be saved by decanting the mixed colour into an airtight container, such as any kitchen receptacle with a lid. With your own mixed colours an airtight lid of cling film will mean you can use the paint again, though you will have to be prepared to remove any hardened paint skin that has formed.

If you have been a conscientious stenciller so far, you will have kept a few of the photocopies you made of the final design. You can now colour these in with your chosen paint. Armed with a facsimile of the finished design, hold it as close as you can get to its final position. Then, by standing back and taking stock, you can make sure you can live with the final effect, which is an exercise well worth the effort.

Applying the stencil

FOR YOUR STENCILLED SCHEME TO ENJOY A long and happy existence, it's important to assess the suitability of the surface to be stencilled. Water-based paints will never adhere properly to an oil-based surface. Though you might be able to coax them to give you a flattish finish, particularly after vigorous rubbing with heavy-duty sandpaper, they will be extremely susceptible to any kind of wear. Oil paint, however, loves nothing more than to be applied directly to surfaces base-coated with water-soluble emulsion paints.

Whatever the technique, it's always a good idea to finish off with a coat or two of varnish to create a tough protective shell. Being such a good shield, varnish is obviously one of the worst surfaces to paint on to.

Emulsion – either matt or vinyl silk – is the most usual and popular paint finish for walls. Being water-based, it will be only too happy to receive an over stencil in any paint finish.

Oil-based paint sold as eggshell, gloss or satin finish, is used for doors, windows and other woodwork. Much tougher than emulsion, it is designed to form a smooth surface to which dirt and water-based paint cannot cling. Craft spray, car spray or oil paint are therefore the only practical choices for stencilling.

Stencilling on varnished wood is best attempted with craft or car spray though oil paint can work if you gently sand the surface to give the paint a rougher texture on which to cling and a very thorough varnishing afterwards to protect it. Bare wood will take any technique. A final coat of varnish will not only make it tougher, it will also add depth to the design.

Stencils can look very effective applied straight on to wallpaper, particularly as a lacy border below a picture rail or a cresting just above a dado. Ordinary wallpaper will take all stencilling techniques, though vinyl papers, with their slippery coated surfaces, will quickly repel just about anything you throw at them. Obviously, embossed or woodchip papers will prove a difficult surface to achieve clean lines on. Kitchen or bathroom tiles

'Broken' colour is a perfect background for stencilling. Colour thinned with water or varnish and distressed with a dry rag creates a mellow texture.

Far right *On large areas such as walls, always leave a small gap between painted patches which you can then fill by bringing wet paint across on the rag to join the edges.*

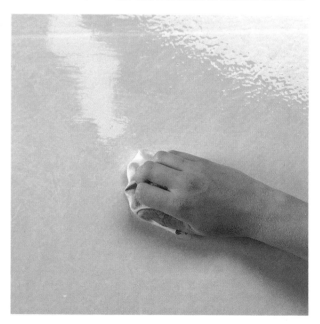

and laminate surfaces or cupboard fronts, though easy to stencil with the sprays, will eventually repel any paint you put on and chip and flake at the slightest knock.

PREPARING YOUR SURFACES

Before stencilling, always make sure that the surface you are going to apply the stencil to is clean and free of dust. Any project will profit from a little time spent gently sanding down the surface with some fine glass or sandpaper. This is particularly important if you are going straight on to varnish or gloss paint. Holes, cracks or irregularities should be filled and smoothed if you want a truly professional finish, though the bumpy, time-mellowed texture of old cottage walls can add pleasing rustic elements to an appropriate stencil scheme, provided the paint is not loose or flaky.

If you are not stencilling straight on to an existing surface but want to create your own coloured base, you must resign yourself to several time consuming and thin coats. Trying to get it all done in one thick layer simply will not work. Always allow time for one coat to dry before applying the next or else you will find the new wet paint removes previous layers as you go along.

Stencilling is always beautifully offset by a slightly clouded paint effect used as a base. This is fairly easy to do and, in simple terms, means thinning down your paint and applying it unevenly with broad strokes from a large paint brush, then rubbing or agitating it with a dry cloth.

Emulsion thinned with water can be extremely messy so protect anything you don't want to break out in a rash of paint spots. It can also be a little tricky on a large wall since you will find areas of the paint drying before you have time to get to them with your cloth. So restrict yourself to working in approximate 90cm (3ft) squares, taking care not to let the paint squares overlap since this will leave you with a darker ridge. Try leaving a small gap as you paint, then quickly filling it in by

bringing the two edges together with a rag and rubbing and smudging them in. This is a very quick antidote to a brightly coloured wall or other surface. A milky-white or cream wash can turn violent primary colours into more muted, restrained tones.

On oil-painted surfaces, some oil pigment or paint in varnish will give you even more flexibility for exciting effects. You will find that the longer drying time of the varnish will allow you to really move the paint around. Rags or natural sponges leave exact imprints allowing the base colour to come through. A vigorous dabbing with a dry stiff brush held at right angles to the surface will give you an all-over stippled finish that's ideal for small objects, mirror frames or door panels. If you find the varnish difficult to handle on larger areas, a little refined linseed oil will slow down the drying time and keep the mixture workable. The same principles can be used after stencilling to create a softer or antiqued effect.

The basic principles of broken colour can be applied to make a wide variety of interesting effects. The different imprints left from sponges, rags or a dry brush all create perfect backgrounds for stencilling.

POSITIONING YOUR STENCIL

There is nothing worse than a stencil that is quite obviously supposed to be bang in the middle of a surface and is quite obviously not. Similarly, a crooked motif or border that starts dropping halfway across a wall can make even grown men cry. Since you have been conscientious enough to find the middle of your design and provide yourself with a straight ruled mid line, there should be no reason why you can't measure the surface and leave a light pencil mark to marry up with the centre mark of your stencil. For smaller flat surfaces, a set square can be used to ensure the centre line is a true right angle. Walls will need a spirit level to give you a true vertical. Since the walls, ceilings and floors of many houses come only close to approximating perfect right angles, use a spirit level to make a line for a repeating border to follow.

One of the cardinal rules of stencilling is to always start in the middle and work outwards. This ensures that the design is correctly balanced within the perimeters of the surface. If you have designed a repeating stencil to fit exactly from corner to corner, then have a gold star. If not, then starting from the middle will mean any funny little fractions or gaps are kept to the less visible perimeters. Though it might go very much against the grain, measuring in metric is infinitely preferable to the complicated eighths or twelfths of unwieldly imperial measurements.

You will now need to fix your stencil quite firmly in place. Small squares of masking tape at

The centre line of the stencil should always be aligned with a measured mark if the stencil is to fit a specific area.

Small squares of masking tape can be used to hold the stencil in position – but try out the masking tape first to make sure it doesn't remove any existing surface paint.

each corner will hold it nice and steady – but try out the masking tape first to make sure it doesn't remove any of the existing surface paint. Drawing pins leave rather permanent little holes and blobs of blue-tack can raise the stencil away from the surface, allowing paint to seep or dribble. By far the best solution is spray adhesive, particularly the sort sold as non-permanent for mounting photographs. Be warned, however, that you will inevitably deliver a good deal of overspray that can settle and stick to anything within range. It is also one of the nastiest things to inhale. So, provided that there isn't too much wind to blow dust and grit on to the sticky surface, you will be best spraying outside. Go for a fine, even coat – the more glue you apply the stickier it is and thus starts becoming

efficient at removing paint. The glue has a tendency to lose its tack as you go along but try to resist the temptation to keep reapplying. Technically, it is a good idea to remove glue from the stencil before reapplying, by rubbing it softly with a cotton wool ball and a little petrol cleaner or lighter fuel. (But don't smoke.)

Spray adhesives will keep every bit of the stencil flat and fixed to the surface and will ensure you get crisp, high definition stencils. They are brilliant at holding delicate filaments in place, but you must be very gentle when peeling the stencil from the surface to avoid damaging the finer cuts. Sadly, spray adhesives could never be considered cheap, but you will find a can extremely useful for a variety of jobs around the home.

For running patterns it is essential to mark out the repeat before you start.

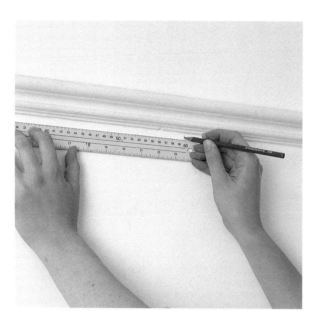

Leave any half repeats or corners until last to minimize damage to the stencil.

APPLYING YOUR STENCIL

Having calculated where the stencil is to go and how many times it is to repeat, make a mental note of any halves or fractions of the design you will need to fit into corners or around light fittings etc. Always make sure you have tackled every inch of an area that takes a full repeat before attempting to bend the stencil to fit into a corner or around an impediment. Bending stencils not only reduces their strength and lifespan, but can also distort the design. Bending the design around a corner is best done in two stages, with time allowed for the first half to dry before applying the stencil to the adjacent surface. You will be surprised how much a corner will disguise inconsistencies or botched repeats, providing the top and bottom correspond with the stencil levels on the neighbouring surface.

Whether using a brush or a sponge, always remove as much excess paint as possible before setting to work. Thoroughly dab the paint on to a piece of newspaper or an uncut part of the stencil until you are left with a crisp, clear imprint of your brush or your sponge. Then, starting in the middle of the largest cut, work back so that by the time you get to the edges, a minimum of paint is being applied. (Fuzzy edges and trickles occur when too much paint builds up at the edge of the cut.) If the design is beginning to look a little insipid by the time you get to the edges, don't worry, as you can always go back over it with subsequent, light layers. But you will be amazed at how visible and crisp the final effect will be once you have removed the stencil. Keeping your brush at right angles to the surface is essential. If it's at an angle you will find stray hairs can easily sneak behind the stencil and mark the wall. Keep a small dish or saucer of water and lots of washing up liquid to hand. If you have small smudges or dribbles, timely application with a cotton bud may be enough to save the day. Often, however, you may find you have to resign yourself to painting out mistakes with a fine brush when the stencilled project is complete and dry.

SPRAY STENCILLING

In most cases when spray stencilling, you will have to make a box mask to stop any problems with overspray. This can often mean you end up working 'blind', as registration or centre marks can be difficult to see. Spray stencilling is a lot more complicated to set up than other techniques where you can more or less launch straight in following a few basic steps, though spray-applying the paint makes up for lost time in preparation. As with brushed or sponged stencils, any build-up of paint near the edge can lead to drops or dribbles, so keep your spray as fine as possible.

If you are looking to re-use a stencil, always make sure it is stored flat. After a heavy duty session, stencils can end up quite soggy. Spray mounting them to glass or ceramic will hold them flat as they dry off and will mean they are easy to remove when dry. Excess paint should be carefully wiped off before storage; a light dusting of talcum powder will absorb any retained moisture.

VARNISHING

The durability of any stencilling project is greatly increased by a coat or two of varnish. Though not really necessary over a high level border stencilled on top of emulsion, varnishing is essential on anything that might receive heavy wear or regular use. On aesthetic grounds, a coat of varnish will bring a bloom to colours that makes them richer and more attractive. High gloss finishes should for the most part be avoided in favour of satin or matt varnishes. All three finishes are available in polyurethane (white spirit soluble) or acrylic (water soluble). Polyurethane or acrylic are both equally good, though, whatever it says on the can, polyurethane is not entirely clear and will yellow the stencil slightly. This can often be a bonus in that it will take the edge off over bright colours and build a little age into the finish. You could take this further still by adding a little oil paint (any of the umbers or siennas work marvellously) well

diluted with turps to the varnish. This will give you a glaze which you can distress with a stiff dry brush before the glaze dries totally to achieve a thoroughly lived-in finish.

Purists will wish to gently sand each coat of varnish with a fine grain glass or sandpaper and build up a series of thin varnish coats. This will get rid of any dust or tiny grit particles that have managed to lodge in the wet varnish. Always stir varnish thoroughly before use because the formulation can settle if left too long on the shelf. Short strokes with a vaguely upright brush will give you a more consistent finish. Yet again, aim for a series of thin coats rather than a thick gloopy layer which may eventually crack or discolour.

Smudged stencils are caused by a build-up of paint at the edges. You can avoid this by starting in the middle of each element and gradually working outwards.

Projects

With your newly acquired stencilling skills, you'll find all the projects that follow easy to make. But don't forget, they are just ideas. Each of the stencil designs featured can be used on absolutely anything you like – just scale them up or down as required. You will be amazed at the results you can achieve!

Mirror frame

You will need:
- Mirror frame of unvarnished, untreated timber
- Fine sandpaper
- Vinyl silk emulsion in pale stone colour
- Pencil
- Ruler
- Manila card, acetate or plan trace
- Scalpel (or cutting blade) and cutting mat
- Spray adhesive
- Yellow Ochre acrylic paint
- Paint kettle or saucer (for mixing paints)
- Bathroom sponge
- Clear polyurethane varnish

For oil-primed surfaces
- Alkyd, craft spray or oil pigment
- White spirit (for cleaning brushes)

This is an excellent project for beginners as it's quick and easy to make. Our starting point was a very simple mirror frame of untreated pine. For such a down-to-earth object we decided to utilize the rough finish of stencilling to create a 'rustic' or 'countrified' look.

Before buying the mirror we checked with the shop that it hadn't been treated or varnished in any way – a varnished timber frame would need more complicated preparation (see p. 35). The frame was lightly sanded first to remove any roughness.

1 Mix a little Yellow Ochre with the emulsion and apply to the base-coated frame with a sponge.

Two coats of vinyl silk emulsion were then applied, followed by some more emulsion mixed with a tint of Yellow Ochre acrylic paint. This new colour was applied in a thin wash and gently distressed to achieve a subtle clouded finish (see p. 34).

While the paint was drying, a classic ivy leaf design was drawn up. The simple outline of the ivy leaf was ideal for a stencil, and the long undulating stalks perfect for decorating tall narrow areas. The position of each leaf and the regular curves of the stalks were carefully calculated to fit into the rectangular frame. After measuring the distance between the leaves and sketching in the stalks, a template was then cut directly from the outline of the leaf. The template was then drawn around to make the design.

The design was stencilled using a bathroom sponge. The chosen colour had a base of acrylic Yellow Ochre to which a good splodge of the original emulsion had been added, to create a closely related, mellow colour balance. After stencilling, the stencil was left to dry, then flipped over to create a mirror image. After a good 12 hours, a couple of coats of matt varnish were used to protect the paint.

2 Lay out the stencil design, using an ivy leaf template. Divide the length of the mirror frame by the length of a leaf and stalk to calculate the number of leaves and stalks that will fit. Then draw around each ivy leaf template and connect each leaf by drawing a curved line for the ivy stalk.

3 Apply Yellow Ochre acrylic through the cut stencil with a bathroom sponge.

Monogrammed box

This is an ideal personalized present – particularly appropriate as a wedding gift, since the initials of the couple can be combined in the monogram. The starting point was a very ordinary little box to which a few coats of Dark Oak varnish had been applied.

The first thing to do was to make an accurate plan of the box lid and then to calculate its centre by joining each corner from the diagonal. With the midpoint calculated, a DIY compass using a thinning piece of string or twine and a map pin gave a perfect circle. If you do this, remember to keep the string as taut as possible. Make sure you leave a little space around the circle so that the design is not cramped on the box lid.

The next stage was to make the monogram, since the size and shape of the letters would affect the size and shape of the border. The letters H and S were traced from a newspaper headline, and their size slightly increased with a photocopier. (The more the letters are interwoven, the more decora-

tive the monogram will become.) Because the box lid was quite small, simple classic letters were used, but made more interesting by making the S curve and snake around the straight lines of the H.

A wreathed circle of reeds and long pointed leaves was chosen for the border. First, a rough sketch was made, following one half of the circle drawn earlier, then, when the right look was achieved, the half was reversed to finish the circle and make a symmetrical, perfectly balanced wreath.

A light spray in a Gold Ochre colour was then applied. Craft spray was chosen for this project because of its suitability for a varnished surface, but a box that has been base-coated in emulsion obviously offers more flexibility in terms of choice of paint. Because the desired finish was one similar to marquetry, where different wood veneers are used to make patterns, a gently broken layer of a Dark Umber colour was then sprayed on to create a feeling of wood grain.

1 Make an accurate plan of the top of the box and find its midpoint by connecting the diagonals from each corner. Using a piece of string and a map pin as shown, to improvise a simple compass, create a circle from the midpoint of the box.

2 Take chosen initials and enlarge them to the required size (see p. 24). Combine them on tracing paper to form your decorative monogram. Then, following the circle in step 1, draw up one side of the wreath border using tracing paper to create a mirror image.

The finished stencil now had a richness and depth to it, but the motif seemed rather isolated, so a pretty border detail was created to edge the perimeter of each face by cutting manila card masks, then using pinking shears to cut a zigzag border a few millimetres in from each edge. The masking required in such cases is time-consuming – particularly since each face can only be sprayed when the previous stencil is dry – but the effect is well worth it. To unify the effect and give further depth to the gold-coloured stencil, the finished box was then given a final coat of the tinted satin varnish originally used to base-coat the box.

3 Having combined the border and the monogram, transferred them to manila card and cut the stencil, mark all areas of the box you are not spraying, and apply a thin coat of Yellow Ochre craft spray. Leave to dry, and spray a second gentle application of Dark Umber, allowing the paint to spatter.

4 Create a sawtooth border on your stencil card with pinking shears and leave the box to dry for a few hours.

5 Apply a final coat of the Dark Oak tinted varnish used to treat the box originally.

Repeating border

You will need:
- An 'egg and dart' design, with at least 4 eggs and 4 darts
- Spirit level
- Tracing paper
- Pencil
- Tape measure
- Manila card, acetate or plan trace
- Scalpel (or cutting blade) and cutting mat
- Warm Grey acrylic paint mixed with a little emulsion
- Brushes
- Flake White acrylic paint
- Clear polyurethane varnish

This decorative border is designed to look like a dado – an architectural device much used up until early this century to protect wall finishes from the damage caused by chair backs. Dados offer many design possibilities, since they can add detail to an otherwise plain room, and can be used to improve the proportions of a low-ceilinged, square space. The traditional height of a dado, based on classical architecture, is exactly one third of the overall height of a room. You can, however, play around with this proportion to suit yourself. Very low ceilinged rooms will seem much higher with a dado a little on the low side, and a high ceiling can be brought down with a tall dado.

The design chosen to define this dado was a simplified 'egg and dart' motif very often used by wallpaper companies for paper borders. Its close repeat means that awkward corners, such as those around a chimney breast, can be easily accommodated, without showing up any missed or botched repeats. The design itself was traced up from a book of classical architectural mouldings, then photocopied to a size that worked well within the space – in this case, 5cm (2in) high. Before setting a line to

1 Trace your design and shade in the 'negative' areas between each egg and dart.

follow around the room, however, the chosen height was checked to see that it cleared the top of any radiators, to allow plenty of room for a clear, crisp finish. The dado line should also not be so high that it passes over the mantle shelf, or directly over the windows.

Coming up with the right dimensions involves a lot of boxing and coxing which, when it comes down to it, is best done by eye. Using a spirit level, a faint pencil line was marked around the area to be stencilled, and the height checked every now and again with a tape measure.

Taking the original traced section, which had

2 Mark a line around the room, using a spirit level. Gently apply Warm Grey acrylic through the stencil. Leave to dry for a few seconds, before applying a second layer at the top of the stencil.

four eggs and four corresponding darts, a separate trace was made with two parallel lines defining the perimeter of the design. This was laid over the original. Having measured the width of the eggs and the darts, right-angled sections between the two lines were then marked. (For this alternate repeat it is essential that if you start with an egg at one end, you finish with a dart at the other.)

This stencil is what's known as 'reversed'. In other words, the design has been used to define the area between the eggs and the darts, to give the motif a more three-dimensional look. The straight upper and lower edge now provided also prevents it from looking messy or isolated on the wall.

The close repeat of the design meant it wasn't really necessary to start in the middle of the wall when applying the stencil. A warm grey was mixed with some of the background colour of the wall, to add a three-dimensional effect, and finished with the same paint as the surrounding wall. Using a stiff dry brush, emulsion was applied along the stencil, leaving as light a finish as possible. The emulsion dried in about 5 minutes, which meant we could then go back to the beginning of each stencil and apply more paint to the top of each cut. This gave a flat, darker area, which, when the stencil was removed, looked like shadow cast between the mouldings.

For the highlight colour, some of the original wall emulsion was mixed with some Flake White acrylic containing just the tiniest dash of complementary red. Working diagonally from bottom right to top left, less and less paint was left on the wall. A final coat of matt varnish was then applied for added protection.

3 Cut a second stencil the same shape as the egg, but ½cm (5mm) smaller all the way round, then, using a dry brush with some Flake White acrylic, highlight the bottom right corner with a dry brush dipped in white acrylic.

The completed border

The bedroom

You will need:
- Bedhead
- Piece of cotton
- Pencil
- Warm Grey acrylic paint
- Terracotta-coloured emulsion
- Fine paintbrush
- Clear polyurethane varnish
- Manila card, acetate or plan trace
- Scalpel (or cutting blade) and cutting mat
- Spray adhesive
- Bathroom sponge

For oil-primed surfaces
- Alkyd, craft spray or oil pigment
- White spirit (for cleaning brushes)

This stencilled bedroom shows just how marvellously flexible stencilling can be. The design is a particularly pretty modern version of the French 18th-century pattern known as 'Toile de Jouy'. It is an intricate and delicate pattern, but the strong lines and emphatic shapes together with the variety of separate motifs have a great deal of scope.

The original idea was to just focus on the bedhead – and possibly the cupboards – and leave the rest to evolve naturally. This is often the best approach, since it means that options can be kept open and decisions made on the hoof. Patterned areas can then be easily balanced with undecorated finishes in the space, and a scheme created from different

Bedhead

1 Calculate central mark of bedhead and central line of stencil. Suspend a pencil from a piece of cotton from the central mark of the bedhead, then offset the stencil from this central mark and apply Warm Grey acrylic, using a bathroom sponge. When dry, re-align central line of stencil to central mark of bedhead and apply terracotta emulsion with a bathroom sponge.

2 Notice how effective using the same stencil twice can be in adding depth to the design.

elements unified by colour and pattern.

The first point of attack was the bedhead. Its central point was calculated, and, using a DIY plumbline made from a piece of cotton and a pencil, gravity gave us a 'true vertical' centre line. A mental note was then made of how high the pillows came – losing the very end of a design behind pillows looks nice and informal, but to mislay more than 40 per cent under linen would look messy and ill-considered. This particular bedhead was made by cutting a piece of MDF (medium-density fibre-board) into a shape that perfectly complemented the motif. The bedhead was then screwed straight into the plaster and given the same paint treatment as the rest of the wall. In this case, it was emulsion, but if you are about to launch into an existing bedhead the chances are that it will be finished in an oil paint, for which you will need to use a spray.

The stencil was aligned with the centre mark, then moved a few millimetres to the left and a little down. To add more interest to the design, a 'drop shadow' effect was created by a light sponge application of a pale warm grey. When this had completely dried, the design was stencilled in a terracotta emulsion to go with the fabric. By re-aligning this stencil to the centre line, the terracotta motif was then centred to the bedhead.

The large design here offered plenty of scope for a wide range of techniques. Different densities of paint add interest and life to a pattern, and a few minutes spent sharpening some of the shapes with a fine paintbrush will leave you with a polished finish. Varnishing is essential on a headboard because it is at risk not only from knocks and scrapes, but from oily heads. In this case, a little Yellow Ochre was added to the varnish for a mellow and antique effect.

A smaller version of the central design was used to add interest to the bedside tables, and the larger version with a spray was used on the lampshades. For the rather plain cupboards, the pretty jug motif from the bedhead design was isolated and photo-

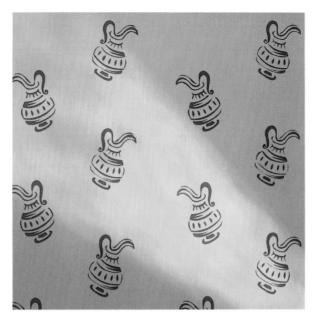

Cupboards
Stencilling an entire wall to look like wallpaper requires a lot of preliminary measuring. Using a plumb line or spirit level, divide the area vertically. The effect works best when, as here, the motif is alternately reversed.

copied until it was small enough to fit. The cupboards had been finished in eggshell paint, and as we wanted to stencil straight on to the cupboards, we had to mix up a new colour in an oil pigment. Alkyd – a relatively new paint – was used because it dries more quickly and has a stiffer texture than ordinary oil-based pigments. The original acrylic colour used for the bedhead was based on Indian Red. You will find that acrylic and oil paints have many colours in common, including Indian Red, which means that different surfaces can have the same coloured stencil.

There was no preset plan for how many jug motifs would be used over the cupboards, or where they would be placed. Having come to the end, there was one jug too many – but, since it had only recently been applied, it was easily removed with a rag soaked in turps.

Decorative frieze

You will need:
- Tracing paper
- Pencil
- Manila card, acetate or plan trace
- Scalpel (or cutting blade) and cutting mat
- Spray adhesive
- Paint kettle or saucer (for mixing paints)
- dark biscuit, dark pink, dusky pink and green-grey emulsion paint
- Bathroom sponge
- Spirit level

This project helps solve one of the most common problems encountered by the interior designer: the contrast between richly coloured and patterned fabrics set against a pale-coloured wall. Often, the patterned fabric of curtains is the only one in the room, so these colours and design need to be carried through to create a more integrated feel to the space. This is best achieved with a stencilled border, or frieze, running below the cornice.

The colour choices for the stencil were relatively easy: dark biscuit, dark pink, light pink and greenish-grey. At first sight, however, the pattern seemed to offer rather too much choice. Although charming, the small curtain motif was too complicated for stencilling; the elongated wreath with its stylized bows was too tall and thin to act as a border, and the fruit bowl, in its entirety, was too busy for a repeated design. The upper half of the fruit bowl, on the other hand, immediately caught the eye as a good starting point for the border. So this element was traced. The grapes, however,

were left out, as they would end up as being too dense. This left a rather nasty gap in the bottom right hand corner which was filled by repeating a few of the flowers from the top of the design. Although almost there, the design now seemed too square, so the elegant curved bow was lifted from the neighbouring motif. The end result was something that was not only attractive, but perfect for a repeating pattern. The shapes were simplified slightly, the filaments sketched in, and the whole thing photocopied several times.

Although this is a four-colour design, only three separate stencils were used. (If you work cleanly and methodically, there is no real limit to the amount of colour you can use through one stencil.) Like all furnishing fabrics, this fabric had a series of small colour registration circles showing each of the colours used to make up the design – a helpful guide when mixing paints. (If you hunt around inside your curtains you will probably find them on an outside seam.) In this case, the elegant biscuit

1 The starting point for the stencil design.

2 Having traced and adapted the fruit bowl motif, add adjacent elements to round off the design.

3 Mix up the tints, referring to the fabric and the colour registration marks on the back of the fabric. Try out each colour on the background wall colour and leave to dry.

colour in the curtains formed the starting point. This was the base colour from which the other colours were created. The biscuit base was put into three pots. To the first were added carefully controlled dribbles of a dusky pink; to the second, grey-green; and to the third a tiny amount of a dirty wine-coloured paint.

All the colours were then put on a photocopy of the design, and matched up in different combinations to suit the different elements in the pattern. The zigzagging lines that followed the contours of the motif to soften changes from colour to colour in the original fabric were retained for the stencil. In the curtains, some of the pattern elements, such as the rim of the grapefruit, the highlights on the apple and the leaves were created by leaving the light base colour blank. Since light stencilling allows much of the base colour to show through, additional shades can be created by applying one colour on to another. Therefore, areas where the green and the pink could be made lighter by being applied over the pale wall colour were marked.

4 Colour in the final photocopy of the design.

5 Trace the outline of each colour on a separate piece of tracing paper.

The final design was then broken down into three colour stencils by tracing the outline of each area of colour, ensuring that the centre lines were accurately marked on each trace.

The first stencil was used for the biscuit colour. The areas where the wall colour was to be used were clearly marked. (If manila card is used, make a V-shaped groove at either side along the horizontal midpoint.) A line was then drawn with a spirit level to follow. At the midpoint of each wall, the position of each stencilled repeat was then marked off, so that we could see where to bend the design to fit around corners.

After finishing the first stencil, the registration grooves were followed with a light pencil line. The other stencils were lined up on these marks and the pencil lines were removed with a rubber.

6 To see if the finished effect works, try each stencil out on a piece of card before applying it to the wall.

7 To ensure that each stencil is correctly registered, cut V-shaped grooves along the centre line of each card. Make a light pencil mark on these V grooves and then line up each subsequent stencil to the mark.

Stencilled stripes

You will need:
- Spirit level
- Pencil
- Rubber
- Low-tack masking tape or manila card
- Spray adhesive
- Calculator
- Set square
- Clear polyurethane varnish
- Refined linseed oil
- Raw Umber oil pigment
- 2 brushes – 1 wet, 1 dry
- Turpentine or white spirit (for cleaning brushes)

Unusual wall finishes below a dado are both popular and extremely effective. Using broadly striped wall papers below dado rails was very common during much of the 19th century, and this effect can be easily reproduced with paint. Vertical stripes are an effective device for increasing the height of a room but can sometimes be a little too bold if used over an entire wall. Restricted to the area below a dado rail, however, they add a note of elegance and increase the feeling of space without overpowering the rest of the scheme.

Dados are often largely obscured by furniture, which means you can afford to be quite daring in your colour combinations if you are striving for a very contemporary look. For this project, however, the colours were kept muted and tonally balanced for a classically elegant look.

Although the following method of painting stripes is not strictly speaking stencilling in its purest form, it uses the same principles. If you have no architectural dado moulding, you will have to draw a spirit line to work to. You will also eventually need to use either a printed paper border or repeating stencil to create a neat finishing line for the stripes. The 'egg and dart' decorative border (see p. 47) is ideal for neatly finishing painted stripes.

Technically speaking, spending some time and effort calculating a stripe that will fit exactly on to each wall should be the first step, but this process involves some rather vicious long division. We felt that since our stripes were in such a subtle shade, they could accommodate being split on corners, though a bolder combination of colours where the stripes are very defined might need greater consideration.

The easiest stripes are those which are equidistant, or which have the same width for both the stripe and the space between.

A spirit level was taken around the room to measure heights and levels, after which a nice stiff piece of mounting card was cut to the width and height of the stripes – it's very important, in such instances, that all the corners are right-angled, so using a set square is the best idea. This card was then used as a template to mark out the stripes around the room, starting from the middle of the wall we felt was most visible. A spirit level was used every now and again to check that the stripes were vertical. Since dark or heavy pencil lines would inevitably show through the finished stripes, minimum pressure was applied with a hard pencil, giving as pale a mark as possible. A piece of manila card cut to shape and held in place with spray adhesive could be used as a mask, though in this case low-tack masking tape was used – trimmed in half so as not to obscure neighbouring stripes. Ordinary masking tape, whatever the manufacturers may claim, can be very good at pulling off

1 Following a level line, mark in the position of each stripe using a cardboard template.

existing paintwork. Low tack masking tape is not difficult to find from a good paint merchant, and is not only re-usable, but also very easy to put on in a straight line.

An oil-based glaze was used, together with half a small tin of matt varnish with a dash of refined linseed oil, and some Raw Umber dissolved in turps. Emulsion could obviously be used, but if, as here, you want to disguise a radiator in the paint scheme, you will need to use oil paint or spray. No amount of coaxing will keep emulsion on a radiator for long.

Having masked a few stripes, the glaze was applied working from the middle of the stripe outwards so that the brush was drier as it hit the tape. Because a slow-drying oil glaze was used, the stripe had to be gone over again with a coarse dry brush, literally dragging the paint downward, keeping the brush at a right angle to the wall. The result was lovely mellow stripes with a delicately 'worn' texture to them. You could, however, successfully use other techniques with rags, sponges or plastic bags to create a texture in the paint. (If when you remove the tape or the manila mask you find the glaze has seeped underneath and smudged, speedy action with a cotton bud soaked in turps will save the day.)

It's always a good idea to start painting in an area that you know will be hidden by a sofa or in a dark corner behind your hi-fi. This will give you an opportunity to gain confidence before tackling the more visible areas such as alcoves on either side of the chimney breast.

Because a varnish-based glaze was used on this project, an additional coat of varnish was not needed. But bear in mind that emulsion stripes are easily scuffed unless they are sealed with a tough matt or satin varnish.

Stencilled stripes – perfect for below a dado rail.

2 Mask the edge of each stripe using either low-tack masking tape or manila card and spray adhesive. Apply the varnish/pigment glaze in short diagonal strokes.

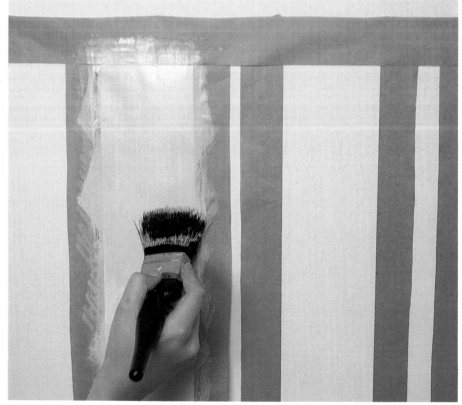

3 While the glaze is still wet, and using a dry brush, drag the pigment in long downward strokes.

The nursery

You will need:
- Manila card, acetate or plan trace
- Scalpel (or cutting blade) and cutting mat
- Spray adhesive
- Scrap paper for masking
- Craft spray or acrylic paints in assorted colours
- Magic marker
- Pen
- Masking tape

Of all the rooms in the house, the stencilled nursery has become an enduring favourite. This is probably down to the fact that nursery stencils at their best are simple and bright. Although complicated stencil schemes of Kate Greenaway figures or locomotives accurately reproduced down to the last piston are undeniably lovely, it's a matter of debate whether such sophistication is appreciated by the room's tiny inhabitants. It's a depressing fact of life that within a few frighteningly short years, anything you stencil in the nursery will be dismissed by its occupant as being 'kiddy'. So, while the children are still young and without the necessary vocabulary to complain, go for bright saturated all-over colours, which tiny new formed eyes do seem to notice and enjoy.

Most nurseries are furnished during the month-by-month countdown to the new arrival, which means that particular attention must be paid to the

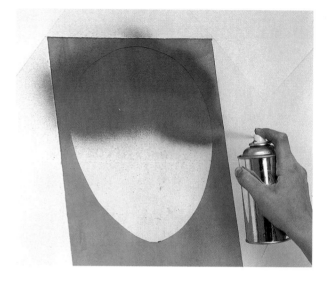

1 Connect the top and bottom of a centre line to form a curved balloon shape, then cut the stencil. Make sure that before spraying through the stencil on to the wall, the surrounding area has been completely masked.

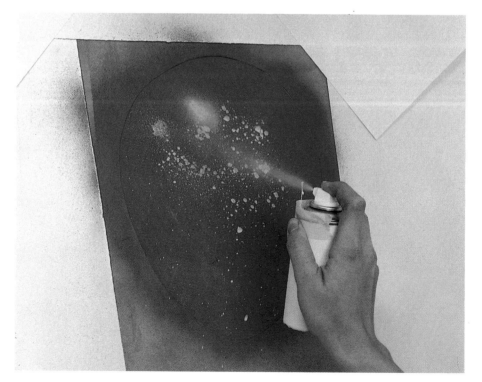

2 When the base colour has dried, spurt spray a second colour by taping a pin to the side of the can so that it interrupts the spray of paint.

3 *A short burst from the white spray gives a lifelike highlight. Draw in the curling balloon string using a black Magic marker.*

The balloon shape used could not be easier – a suitable curve joins the top and bottom of a centre line, which is then traced to provide a symmetrical mirror image. By keeping the paint spray fine, the stencil is quite transparent, allowing the overlap between the two balloons to create a new colour. The same effects are possible with a dry application of emulsion or acrylic paint.

To give the balloons added interest and life, a contrast colour was 'spurt' sprayed. (Basically, this means taping a pin or needle to the top of the can so that it directly interrupts the spray of paint, resulting in larger blobs and spots of colour.) A white spray was then used to create a highlight that made the balloons round and rubbery. The curving curling strings were added with a square-nibbed permanent marker.

The metal toy chest was first sprayed a Sky Blue, then the fluffy clouds were sprayed on through a simple cloud-shaped stencil. To add a little more depth, some of the clouds received the lightest possible spray while others took several coats to make them dense. For a really airy effect, the same principle could be applied to the walls. Start with a blue emulsion that has a faint suggestion of violet and vary the denseness and size of the clouds by only spraying the edge of the stencil on some to give a real feeling of space.

This type of random project is ideal for tackling a little at a time. More than one nursery has remained incomplete at the arrival of its new occupant, as the task became an increasing burden to the heavily pregnant stenciller. The beauty of this scheme is that there is no definitive finishing line – you could find balloons appearing anywhere!

dangers of paint fumes and ladders. The nursery shown here is bold, simple and designed in such a way that it can be completed over an extended period. In order that the stencil can be applied over a variety of surfaces with little time-consuming preparation, craft sprays have been used. This means that proper ventilation and a good face mask are essential. It may also be a good idea to quickly check with the manufacturers about safety. Although craft sprays are not theoretically harmful, car sprays could be potentially very dangerous if you are pregnant.

The kitchen

You will need:
- Manila card, acetate or plan trace
- Scalpel (or cutting blade) and cutting mat
- Spray adhesive
- Bathroom sponge
- Acrylic paints in assorted colours
- Heat-resistant varnish
- Paintbrush
- White spirit (for cleaning brush)
- Saucer (for mixing paints)

After the rather clinical-looking kitchens of the last decade, it's been a relief to see a friendlier look resurfacing in recent kitchen designs. One of the problems is that since wallpaper is rarely advisable in an area where steam and heat are constantly produced, the potential for introducing pattern and accents of colour in a kitchen using conventional methods is quite limited. This makes the hardwearing finish of stencilling ideal for adding some life and interest to this room. Having said that, however, kitchen stencils must be limited to surfaces that are receptive to paint if you want the designs to survive. There is no paint in the world that will stay looking good and still adhere to modern laminates, and painting on ceramic tiles should only be attempted with specialist tile paint, which is too runny for stencilling. Timber-fronted kitchen units will, however, take stencilled designs that will endure most things if properly varnished. If, as here, your cabinet fronts are faced in laminate, however, concentrate instead on stencilling the door panels or walls.

The stencilled kitchen chosen here uses an appropriately culinary stencil with a bold outline and simple shapes that are in keeping with the countrified feel of the units. The form of each object is boldly blocked in with a rough-textured application of paint using a dryish sponge.

When completely dry, the detail is added freehand with a paintbrush. This may sound daunting, but is, in fact, less complicated than cutting a series of different stencils for each colour. As long as you take time to create a prototype to follow, as with the frieze (see p. 53), you won't go wrong. The

1 Cut the outline shape of the stencil design and apply a textured coat of pale ochre acrylic paint.

rustic look of this design is actually improved by irregularity and roughness.

Stencils used on a kitchen wall should always be varnished. Here, the stencilled baskets have received several coats of varnish to protect them, and the stencil design on the tray has been treated with a heat-resistant varnish to combat hot mugs or plates.

As in the nursery and bedroom, this scheme benefits from an 'organic' approach that offers tremendous scope for the stenciller. By varying the scale of the motif to correspond with the object to be stencilled, the design can crop up anywhere and allows for a series of small-scale, quick projects.

2 Following your prototype on cardboard, tint the various different elements in the design using watered-down acrylic paints over the original stencil.

3 Apply several coats of heat-resistant varnish to anything that may come in contact with hot plates or mugs.

The stencilled kitchen.

Projects

A Mexican-style bathroom

You will need:
- Manila card, acetate or plan trace
- Scalpel (or cutting blade) and cutting mat
- Pencil
- Tracing paper
- Coarse sandpaper
- Spray adhesive
- Acrylic paints in assorted colours
- Warm Terracotta matt emulsion
- Matt spray varnish
- Clear polyurethane varnish
- Newspaper

Bathrooms are best approached with a degree of whimsy and fun. Usually tiny, they are rarely of any architectural merit, and are inhabited for only a limited time each day. Many bathrooms, as here, can have a very cold feel, due to large expanses of shiny white ceramic and direct overhead lighting. A strong – perhaps even daring – approach to colour offers instant improvement, and an ideal opportunity to explore a particular theme.

In this bathroom, the bright warm colours and primitive patterns of Mexico have been used as a starting point. The architecture in this space is so disjointed that the mellow terracotta paint finish has been extended to the ceiling to create a feeling of warmth and colour. The bold wall and ceiling Zigarat stencils have been 'weathered' by rubbing with a coarse grain sandpaper and the surfaces have been varnished for extra protection.

Thinned-down emulsion was rubbed into the grain of the untreated wooden shelf front which was suspended from the ceiling to clear the sloping wall in this attic room. Additional detail was provided by upholstery nails. The stencilled motif was kept as rough and splodgy as possible in colours derived from the Mexican pottery on the shelves.

The colourful collection of terracotta flower pots was stencilled with brightly hued acrylic paints. They could just as easily have been handpainted, since acrylics have the advantage of drying quickly. They are also opaque enough to cover up mistakes or changes of mind. Having given the pots an emulsion finish, a large cone shape was made with a piece of newspaper. The flower pot was then placed inside, and the top and the bottom of the pot traced with felt tip pen. By carefully undoing the cone, a template was left that fitted the flower pot snugly. The stencil was taken from this shape.

It's far easier when stencilling a curved and tapering object to make a stencil that fits like a glove in this way – it means that the paint is less likely to smudge or seep. After a little freehand detailing and a couple of coats of gloss varnish, these pots look just like Mexican ceramics. But bear in mind that they will be unlikely to survive very long outside without several coats of yacht varnish.

The stencilled window solves a common problem. In bathrooms, it's naturally a very good idea to have glass which lets in light, while still being

Walls *Having colour-washed the walls with a terracotta matt emulsion, apply the Zigarat and star stencil with a bathroom sponge, using an opaque layer of the background wall colour between the surface. Distress the surface with coarse grain sandpaper.*

opaque enough to prevent you from being seen. Obscure, or textured, glass is rarely attractive, and sandblasted glass is very expensive. On the other hand, matt car spray, when sprayed directly on to glass, gives a very plausible sandblasted effect. It is also durable and practical enough for most windows.

For this window, a variety of star shapes were cut, together with the odd Mexican Zigarat. The window frame was masked, and the motifs stuck to the glass with spray adhesive. The window was then gently sprayed (you will need to wear a mask for this, as the fumes are particularly unpleasant). This technique can be used for a variety of applications. If you prefer a Victorian-inspired bathroom, ordinary paper doilies will give a lace-like finish while leaves attached to the glass with a PVA adhesive will give you a ready-made forest glade.

Panes of glass and mirrors can be bordered with the simple use of masking tape and a straight line. For example, a particularly elegant window above a front door can be stencilled with the number of the house.

To do this, simply trace the existing brass number from the front door and make a mask from manila card. Then use a masking tape border to create a clear frame around the pane. One of the joys of this technique is that when direct sunlight streams straight through the stencilled glass, the unsprayed areas creating the motif are projected perfectly on to the opposite wall.

Shelf *Apply thinned-down emulsion straight into the grain of the untreated timber and overstencil using bright primitive colours.*

Household items *Many interesting effects can be achieved by using a variety of household items as a mask for your spray stencil pattern. Use paper doilies for lace-like effects, leaves for a forest glade – even large paper clips can create interesting effects.*

Pots Make a large cone shape from a sheet of newspaper, scrap paper or tracing paper. Follow the top and bottom edges of the flower pot with a pencil. Carefully unwrap the paper, and you will have an exact template of the flower pot from which you can derive your stencil.

Window By using matt spray varnish, various effects similar to sandblasted glass can be achieved on windows. This is an easy- to-achieve and good-looking alternative to textured or opaque glass bathroom windows.

Gift ideas

You will need:

Wrapping paper
- Brown paper
- Gold craft spray
- Disco body and hair spray
- Manila card, acetate or plan trace
- Scalpel (or cutting blade) and cutting mat
- Light mount card for gift tags

Photograph frame and album
- As for Wrapping paper (except for disco spray)
- Glue

Place mats
- Hardboard
- Jigsaw
- White emulsion paint
- Pale Blue acrylic paint
- Manila card, acetate or plan trace
- Scalpel (or cutting blade) and cutting mat
- Acrylic varnish
- Blue carbon paper
- Soft pencil
- Fixative spray
- Heat-resistant varnish
- Blue felt
- PVA adhesive

There can be no doubt that actually making a Christmas or birthday present gives more satisfaction, and gains more Brownie points than simply popping into the nearest department store. The flexibility of stencilling also means you can come up with a variety of gifts for very little money.

Wrapping paper *With the price of wrapping paper being so extortionate, stencilling your own makes financial sense, as well as being great fun. It also means you can choose one particular colour or design them, relating all the presents under your Christmas tree to that particular year's decoration. Here, ordinary brown paper has been used with spray stencilled stars. The gold craft spray used has been made even more twinkly by spraying glitter spray (normally reserved for the disco) through the same stencil. (Disco spray comes in a variety of glittery finishes that are non-permanent. It can be sprayed on Christmas trees or used on white linen tablecloths without permanently marking the fabric.) The co-ordinating gift tags have been mounted on light card.*

Photograph album and frame *The photograph album itself has been covered in a heavy paper which was first stencilled and then varnished. This was very simple to do. First, the album was placed on the paper, then the sides, top and bottom of the paper were folded in. The corners were then cut away and two thin V-shaped grooves cut either side of the spine. The cut corners of the cover were then stuck to each other.*

The same stencil used on the album cover has also been applied to a precut picture mount bought at an art shop, and bordered with a gold pen.

Wastepaper bin
- Bin
- Manila card, acetate or plan trace
- Scalpel (or cutting blade) and cutting mat
- High-gloss varnish tinted with Burnt Umber
- Raw Umber

Lampshade
- Lampshade
- Manila card, acetate or plan trace
- Scalpel (or cutting blade) and cutting mat
- Oil paint
- Clear polyurethane varnish
- Soft thin brush with long bristles

Tablecloth
- Plain tablecloth
- Oil pastel colours
- Manila card, acetate or plan trace
- Scalpel (or cutting blade) and cutting mat
- Spray adhesive

Chimney board
- Manila card, acetate or plan trace
- Scalpel (or cutting blade) and cutting mat
- Chosen paints
- Spray adhesive

Placemats *The placemats were cut to size with a jigsaw from hardboard and given several coats of white emulsion. A Pale Blue glaze followed straight on to the base painting, and before it dried, was 'distressed' with a lightweight plastic bag. The subtle blue stencil was applied quite roughly. With blue carbon paper stuck to the back of the original drawing, the outlines and details were then traced with a thick, soft pencil. The mat was then sprayed with a fixative spray from an art shop (though aerosol hairspray would do). Care had to be taken at this stage since too much spray might have caused the carbon lines to bleed, so the applications were kept light and thin. A final coat of heat-resistant varnish and some blue felt stuck to the reverse with PVA adhesive finished the set of mats off perfectly.*

Wastepaper bin *The wooden wastepaper bin has been treated to an elegant new identity, inspired by 18th-century 'Boulle-Work'. Boulle-work, or brass and tortoiseshell wear, was much prized as a rich finish for furniture in the 18th century. In this case, the bin was first sprayed with gold paint. A reverse stencil was then used to mask the metallic base colour and a slodgy effect applied over the exposed areas using high-glass varnish tinted with Burnt Umber. While the varnish was still wet, patches of undiluted Raw Umber were worked in and the whole surface softly stroked with a dry brush to merge the pigment into the varnish. The gold base colour shining through the translucent tinting gives a plausible imitation of natural tortoiseshell.*

Chimney board This is the pièce de résistance. It was cut from a sheet of MDF and stencilled with what must now be a familar design scaled up through photocopying. A little time was then spent finishing off the design with some freehand detailing. Chimney boards are an extremely attractive solution to black and bare empty fire grates and were much loved in the 18th century. Here, a small, right-angled prop fixed to the back of the board keeps it upright, and, as a final touch, a dark tinted varnish gives it a mellow antiqued finish.

Lampshade The lampshade stencil was cut using the same technique as on the flower pots (p. 69), although this time, rather than stencilling the design, the cut-out pattern was used as a guide for freehand painting. This meant that the motif could be done in oil paint mixed with a little varnish which becomes transparent when light passes through it. Stencilling with oil and varnish on to paper or silk mounted on paper shades can end up being very messy. Use a soft brush with long bristles to ensure an even application of paint. Spray, acrylic and emulsion stencils can be used on lampshades, but will not give the same beautiful translucency as stencils using varnish and oil paint.

Tablecloth As a rule, stencilled fabrics are not entirely successful if they are frequently used or washed. This pretty cloth for a small lamp table is unlikely to get much wear or get terribly dirty, so the first stencil from the book was used as a border. Rather than using conventional paint, however, which dries stiff on fabric, or expensive and difficult to find fabric paints, oil pastels from an art shop were used. These give a very pleasant sketchy crayon effect that works very well on cotton. Since you will be rubbing the stencil quite hard with your crayon, you will need to stretch the fabric taut, and anchor the stencil firmly before starting, otherwise the material may crease, leaving small lines in the design. The pastels can be made permanent on the cotton by ironing with a warm to hot iron through the back of the fabric on to paper kitchen towel. This will melt and soak up the oil medium, leaving the pigment permanently in the fabric. Fabrics stencilled like this must not be dry cleaned, but can be machine-washed on a cool setting.

*T*emplates

The Bedhead (p. 50)

The Bedhead (p. 50)

Repeating border (p. 47)

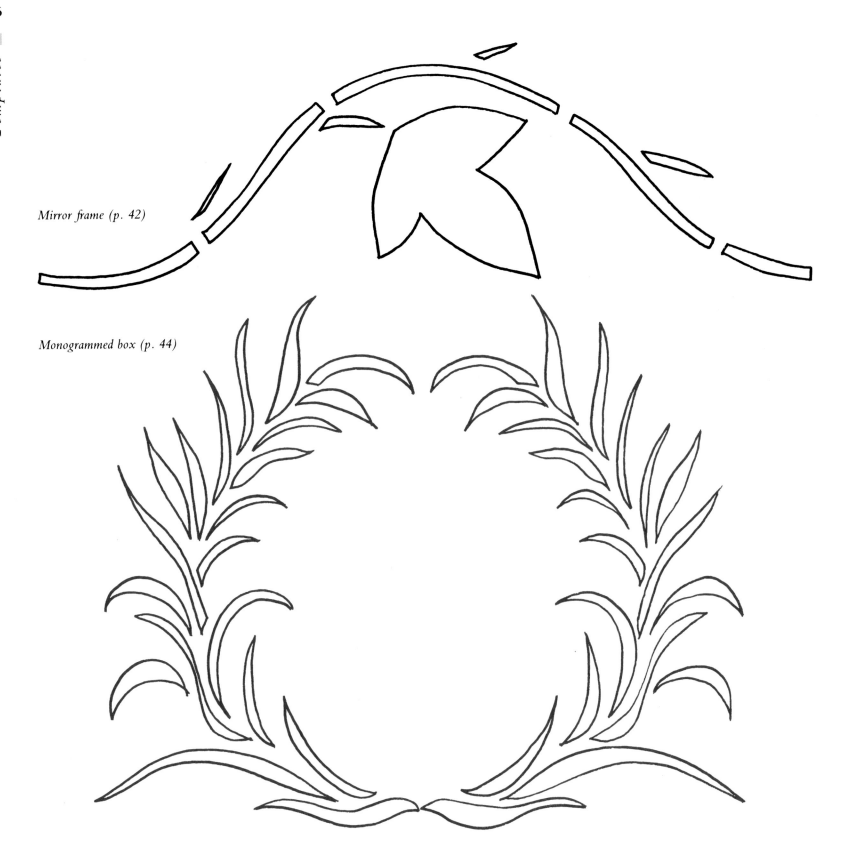

Mirror frame (p. 42)

Monogrammed box (p. 44)

Kitchen (p. 66) (reduced to 75%)

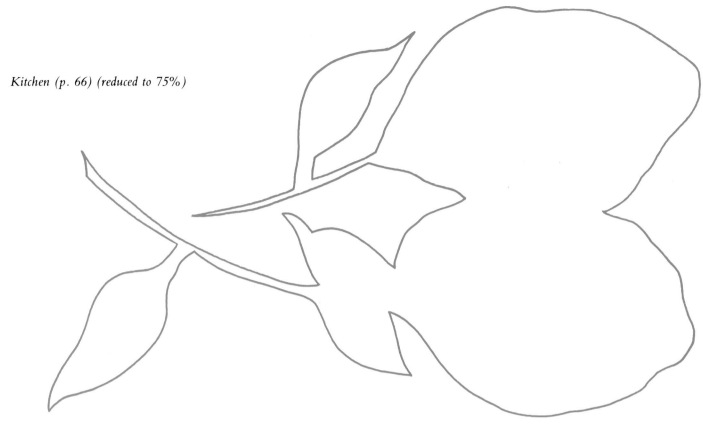

Gift ideas/wastepaper bin (p. 72) (reduced to 75%)

Suppliers

All fabrics used for stencil designs are available from:

Borderline Fabrics
1 Munro Terrace
London SW10 0DL
Tel: 071 823 3567

For stockists and information on many of the materials and equipment used, contact:
Winsor & Newton
Whitefriars Avenue
Wealdstone
Harrow HA3 5RH
Tel: 081 427 4343

For information or advice on craft sprays, contact:
Edding (UK) Ltd
Merlin Centre
Acrewood Way
St Albans
Herts AL4 OJY
Tel: 0727 846 688

Papers and Paints
4 Park Walk
London SW10 0AD
Tel: 071 352 8626

Additional fabrics used were from:
Jason Da Souza
42 Queensland Road
London N7
Tel: 071 607 6755

The authors gratefully acknowledge the help of the following:
Ms Kerry Rew, Edding (UK) Ltd, Mr Jason Da Souza, Ms. Melina Da Souza, Ms. Emma Pierce, Winsor & Newton, Borderline (Cydney Barker and Sally Baring), Mrs Jacqeline Llewelyn-Bowen, Mrs Stephanie Hall, Mrs Diana Wright, Felicity Binyon, Ben and Sara Stocks, Pete Hampel, Julian Stocks, the Gilchrists, Davina Denman, Guy Butterwick, Sarah Bouchier, Serisa Hearn and Henrietta Watson.

Index